# THE URBANE
and other fab crea. ___

# The
# URBANE FOX
## and other fab creatures

TOWYN MASON

(after Phaedrus)

*with illustrations by the author*

*Produced in association with the
Highgate Literary & Scientific Institution,
to which profits from the sale of the book will be donated*

*Published by FeedARead*

# Contents

# Hi!

Early in the new millennium, the modern revival of interest in Antiquity received a novel boost in Highgate, a suburb of north London rich in history and known for its posh houses and numerous pubs. As a six-week experiment, a course cheekily called *Latin for Pleasure* was added to the further education programme of the Highgate Literary & Scientific Institution, a fine early-Victorian establishment which, in the age of email familiarity, has neatly restyled itself Hi. Twelve years later the course is a regular part of the programme and is fully subscribed.

The course was the idea of Isabel Raphael, retired headteacher of Channing School just round the corner from the Institution and before that, in the early 1960s, the school's head of Classics. Some grounding in Latin is needed – typically those attending have studied it up to at least the old O level standard, though in most cases a long time ago – and Isabel chooses texts from Latin writers, adds a vocabulary list, and guides the class through them. Latin without the pain.

But it's not all "veni, vidi, vici". Virgil, Horace and Ovid, Cicero, Tacitus and Pliny junior – most of the golden literati of ancient Rome have had their turn at the table, as well as medieval figures like Abélard and the journalist-manqué monk who so vividly reported the murder of Thomas Becket. Then one day Isabel brought in a few poems by Phaedrus – not in the front rank of Latin letters but a poet noted for turning Aesop into verse 2,000 years ago. An unforeseen consequence was the English versions that follow.

Some of these appeared in the June 2012 issue of *C A News*, the Classical Association's twice-yearly journal. Illustrations have been added and the whole collection published and put on sale with the intention of passing on all profits to the Institution. So high five for Hi Phaedrus!

Classical Latin poetry famously does not rhyme. It's all about metre. Phaedrus used a metrical form called *senarius*, which was favoured by comic playwrights. These translations/adaptations are written in rhyming pentameter couplets which, it is hoped, will be thought to suit the sardonic, often conversational style of poems that contain more fun than profundity and don't take themselves too seriously.

One other translation point: there are some cases of gender reassignment in the text. The Latin words for many animal species, including fox, frog, snake and stork, are feminine, whereas in English the male is favoured, and that is how they appear in the English versions of the poems, except when it is clear the female of the species is meant.

The texts of the poems are taken from *Fables of Phaedrus: a selection* edited by the Rev R H Chambers and published by George Bell & Sons in 1906.

TM
December 2013

# Don't be dumb; keep mum!

Some people are plain suckers for
fine words,
No matter these may just be "for
the birds".

Like a certain crow, who one day sees
Left on a window ledge a piece of cheese.
He grabs it and then flies to a high branch
To eat in peace and quiet his free lunch.
An urbane fox who's watched this from below
Sits up and calls: "Hey, babe, you're quite a crow!
What plumage, and what style – I kid you not,
Star quality's the name for what you've got.
Listen, babe, if only you could sing,
In Birdland they'd be calling you The King!"
"Who, me, can't sing?" the crow thinks, "what a cheek!
I'll show him". And he opens wide his beak.
The cheese falls out, of course, and in a trice
Is snapped up by the fox, who chuckles: "Nice!"
Flattered, tricked and left without a crumb
The crow moans: "How could I have been so DUMB?"


QUI SE LAUDARI GAUDET VERBIS SUBDOLIS,
SERA DAT POENAS TURPES POENITENTIA.

CUM DE FENESTRA CORVUS RAPTUM CASEUM
COMESSE VELLET, CELSA RESIDENS ARBORE,
VULPES HUNC VIDIT, DEINDE SIC COEPIT LOQUI:
≪O QUI TUARUM, CORVE, PENNARUM EST NITOR!
QUANTUM DECORIS CORPORE ET VULTU GERIS!
SI VOCEM HABERES, NULLA PRIOR ALES FORET.≫
AT ILLE, STULTUS DUM VULT VOCEM OSTENDERE,
EMISIT ORE CASEUM, QUEM CELERITER
DOLOSA VULPES AVIDIS RAPUIT DENTIBUS.
TUM DEMUM INGEMUIT CORVI DECEPTUS STUPOR.
  (1:XIII).

# Be not puffed up

O little people: puffed-up imitation
Of the great brings only swift deflation.

A frog looked up one day and noticed, grazing
In the field, a massive bull. "Amazing!
Wannabee like him!" he thought. And so,
Breathing deeply he began to grow
In size, then asked his watching children: "Hey,
That bull, am I now bigger'n him?" "No way",
They answered. Then he had another go,
Puffing strenuously. "And now?" "Er, no."
Furious, he strove yet harder than before
Till BANG! — he blew apart and was no more.

INOPS, POTENTEM DUM VULT IMITARI, PERIT.

IN PRATO QUONDAM RANA CONSPEXIT BOVEM
ET TACTA INVIDIA TANTAE MAGNITUDINIS
RUGOSAM INFLAVIT PELLEM: TUM NATOS SUOS
INTERROGAVIT, AN BOVE ESSET LATIOR.
ILLI NEGARUNT. RURSUS INTENDIT CUTEM
MAIORE NISU ET SIMILI QUAESIVIT MODO,
QUIS MAIOR ESSET. ILLI DIXERUNT BOVEM.
NOVISSIME INDIGNATA DUM VULT VALIDIUS
INFLARE SESE, RUPTO IACUIT CORPORE.
  (1:XXIV)

# Saving your skin

You're deep in dudu? Don't think all is lost;
Try getting out at someone else's cost.
A careless fox fell down a well. Bad luck,
Because he quickly realised he was stuck.
A thirsty goat turned up and said: "Please tell
Me, sir, about the water in this well.
Is it sweet and is there plenty of it?"
"Sure, my friend, just come on in, you'll love it!
I could go on drinking it all day!"
Replied the wily fox, seeing a way
To extricate himself. The bearded one
Jumped in, but before you could say "gone"
The fox was out, free in a single bound.
So how did he contrive this turnaround?
He simply used the goat's horns as a ladder,
Leaving the goat wiser – yeah, and sadder.

HOMO IN PERICLUM SIMUL AC VENIT CALLIDUS,
REPERIRE EFFUGIUM QUAERIT ALTERIUS MALO.
CUM DECIDISSET VULPES IN PUTEUM INSCIA
ET ALTIORE CLAUDERETUR MARGINE,
DEVENIT HIRCUS SITIENS IN EUNDEM LOCUM;
SIMUL ROGAVIT, ESSET AN DULCIS LIQUOR
ET COPIOSUS? ILLA FRAUDEM MOLIENS:
≪DESCENDE, AMICE; TANTA BONITAS EST AQUAE,
VOLUPTAS UT SATIARI NON POSSIT MEA.≫
IMMISIT SE BARBATUS. TUM VULPECULA
EVASIT PUTEO, NIXA CELSIS CORNIBUS,
HIRCUMQUE CLAUSO LIQUIT HAERENTEM VADO
   (4:IX).

# Peacock blues

"Unjust discrimination, that's what I
Am claiming," cried a peacock, "which is why
I've come to this tribunal to complain."
"So," said the judge presiding, "please explain
In what respect you've been unfairly treated."
"Frankly," said the peacock, "I feel cheated.
Every kind of bird, whether friend or
Foe, admires me rightly for my splendour.
Yet when I try to sing they fall about
Laughing, and just tell me 'cut it out!'
Nightingales can warble tunefully;
Why am I denied this faculty?
Basic birdsong rights, that's my demand."
The judge responded: "On the other hand,
With your dazzling hues and gem-like plumage,
Don't the other birds all do you homage?
Isn't that sufficient consolation?"
"Nah", the peacock muttered in frustration,
"What you mean is 'tough, you've got no voice;
Get over it, 'cos there's no other choice."
"Well," said the judge, "we've each got our own gift
From nature. Yours is beauty. Up aloft
The eagle symbolises power in flight.
And as for singing, yes, indeed, you're right:
The nightingale's unbeatable. But even
The crow has certain talents, like the raven.
So make of what you've got the best fist,
Instead of envying others. Case dismissed!"

PAVO AD IUNONEM VENIT INDIGNE FERENS,
CANTUS LUSCINII QUOD SIBI NON TRIBUERIT;
ILLUM ESSE CUNCTIS AVIBUS ADMIRABILEM,

SE DERIDERI, SIMUL AC VOCEM MISERIT.
TUNC CONSOLANDI GRATIA DIXIT DEA:
«SED FORMA VINCIS, VINCIS MAGNITUDINE;
NITOR SMARAGDI COLLO PRAEFULGET TUO
PICTISQUE PLUMIS GEMMEAM CAUDAM EXPLICAS.»
«QUO MI," INQUIT, "MUTAM SPECIEM, SI VINCOR
  SONO?»
«FATORUM ARBITRIO PARTES SUNT VOBIS DATAE:
TIBI FORMA, VIRES AQUILAE, LUSCINIO MELOS,
AUGURIUM CORVO, LAEVA CORNICE OMINA.
OMNESQUE PROPRIIS SUNT CONTENTAE DOTIBUS.»
NOLI ADFECTARE QUOD TIBI NON EST DATUM,
DELUSA NE SPES AD QUERELAM RECIDAT.
  (3:XVIII)

## Sad rags

If you think dressing up can make you posh,
Then think again, 'cos that's a load of tosh!
What lad from a bog standard comp could don
Enough glad rags to fool the Bullingdon?
So hear this tale of sad humiliation.

A jackdaw with ideas above his station
Came across some feathers on the ground
Shed by a peacock. "Hey, guess what I've found!"
He tweeted, putting on this finery.
"I'm feeling like I've won the lottery!
*OK! Hello!* here I come!" And off
He went, convinced he looked a proper toff.
Ignoring his old mates, the self-made snob
Gatecrashed an A-list party to hobnob
With true-blue bird celebs. It cost him dear.
"Who's this upstart? Get him out of here!"
They cried, for they immediately saw through him.
Stripping off his plumes they promptly threw him
Out. So, bruised in body and in mind,
He slunk back in disgrace to his own kind.
But having failed to join the bird beau monde
He found that now he was in turn disowned
By those he had so lately spurned. Said one:
"Serves you right, it's your own fault, my son.
Stop chasing after things you haven't got;
Get a life and put up with your lot".

NE GLORIARI LIBEAT ALIENIS BONIS
SUOQUE POTIUS HABITU VITAM DEGERE,
AESOPUS NOBIS HOC EXEMPLUM PRODIDIT.

TUMENS INANI GRACULUS SUPERBIA,
PENNAS PAVONI QUAE DECIDERANT SUSTULIT
SEQUE EXORNAVIT. DEINDE CONTEMNENS SUOS
SE INMISCUIT PAVONUM FORMOSA GREGI.
ILLI INPUDENTI PENNAS ERIPIUNT AVI
FUGANTQUE ROSTRIS. MALE MULCATUS GRACULUS
REDIRE MAERENS COEPIT AD PROPRIUM GENUS;
A QUO REPULSUS TRISTEM SUSTINUIT NOTAM.
TUM QUIDAM EX ILLIS, QUOS PRIUS DESPEXERAT:
«CONTENTUS NOSTRIS SI FUISSES SEDIBUS
ET QUOD NATURA DEDERAT VOLUISSES PATI,
NEC ILLAM EXPERTUS ESSES CONTUMELIAM
NEC HANC REPULSAM TUA SENTIRET CALAMITAS».
   (1:III)

# Cat's cradle

Three lots of lodgers settled in an oak tree.
At the top an eagle built an eyrie
And hatched a little family of eaglets.
At the base a wild sow with her piglets
Chose a spot where they could play and wallow,
While halfway up a cat found a hollow
In which to live and rear her own litter.
One persistent thought, though, would not let her
Rest: might the outcome of her labour
Be at risk from one or other neighbour?
Reality being, as she saw it, harsh,
She ventured on a dastardly démarche.
Climbing to the eagle's nest she cried:
"Woe! Woe! Twice woe may soon betide
Both you and, I'm afraid, poor little me!
That boarish mob below are wickedly
Digging at the roots of this great oak
To bring it down, so they can at a stroke
Have all our young ones for their delectation."
Thus she left in shock and desperation
Neighbour Number One, then told the sow:
"Calamity! Beware! Your piglets now
Are in grave danger! If you take them out
To forage, then you'd best be in no doubt
That eagle in the nest up there will pounce
And grab them. Trust me, they won't stand a chance."
Leaving also now, consumed by fear,
The sow, she went back to her own safe lair,
From whence at night she surreptitiously
Slipped out to hunt, then ostentatiously
Stayed put during daytime and pretended
She dared not leave her own young unattended.
Thus so craftily did she inveigle

The sow below her and, above, the eagle,
They lapsed into a siege mentality,
Resigned to what seemed their fatality.
Needless to say, confined at home unfed,
They duly starved and ended up dead –
Though for the cat and kittens the deceased
Furnished a most palatable feast.
Which goes to show how two-faced plausible
Deceivers can run rings around the gullible.

AQUILA IN SUBLIMI QUERCU NIDUM FECERAT;
FELES CAVERNAM NANCTA IN MEDIA PEPERERAT;
SUS NEMORIS CULTRIX FETUM AD IMAM POSUERAT.
TUM FORTUITUM FELES CONTUBERNIUM
FRAUDE ET SCELESTA SIC EVERTIT MALITIA.
AD NIDUM SCANDIT VOLUCRIS: «PERNICIES», AIT,
«TIBI PARATUR, FORSAN ET MISERAE MIHI;
NAM FODERE TERRAM QUOD VIDES COTIDIE
APRUM INSIDIOSUM, QUERCUM VULT EVERTERE,
UT NOSTRAM IN PLANO FACILE PROGENIEM OPPRIMAT».
TERRORE OFFUSO ET PERTURBATIS SENSIBUS
DEREPIT AD CUBILE SETOSAE SUIS:
«MAGNO», INQUIT, «IN PERICLO SUNT NATI TUI;
NAM, SIMUL EXIERIS PASTUM CUM TENERO GREGE,
AQUILA EST PARATA RAPERE PORCELLOS TIBI».
HUNC QUOQUE TIMORE POSTQUAM CONPLEVIT LOCUM,
DOLOSA TUTO CONDIDIT SESE CAVO.
INDE EVAGATA NOCTU SUSPENSO PEDE,
UBI ESCA SE REPLEVIT ET PROLEM SUAM,
PAVOREM SIMULANS PROSPICIT TOTO DIE.
RUINAM METUENS AQUILA RAMIS DESIDET;
APER RAPINAM VITANS NON PRODIT FORAS.
QUID MULTA? INEDIA SUNT CONSUMPTI CUM SUIS,
FELISQUE CATULIS LARGAM PRAEBUERUNT DAPEM.
QUANTUM HOMO BILINGUIS SAEPE CONCINNET MALI,
DOCUMENTUM HABERE STULTA CREDULITAS POTEST.
   (2:IV)

# The Bog Society

When freedom turns into a free-for-all
Solid citizens are apt to call
For something to be done. "We cannot stand
By idly", they declare. "An iron hand
Is what we need." And so they put in place
A strongman to control the populace.
Too late they see this was a big mistake;
The new dictator shows he means to make
His power felt, imposing discipline
To which they are unused, so they begin
To rue what they have done, to no avail.
Here, then, is a cautionary tale.

"Enough already!" wailed the frogs in chorus,
Flopping round their murky swamp. "Before us
Filth and squalor's all that we can see;
Croaking is our bog society.
Someone in charge is what we want, to give
A lead – some sort of chief executive."
And so they asked the top authority
To let them have some civic dignity.
But he just laughed: "Why should I waste my time

On losers living up to their eyes in slime?"
Instead he sent a totem pole by air
Freight, whose dreadful aspect put the fear
Of God among the tribe of frogs. None would
For many a day go close to where it stood,
Till one who chanced to pop up alongside
Gave it the once-over and then cried:
"Hey guys! We've been made fools of, come and see!"
At which the others, fearless suddenly,
Raced up to join him and began to vent
Their anger on the useless monument,
Beating and abusing it. They then
Resolved to go and try their luck again.
They pleaded: "Please, we'd like a proper boss;
The last one, with respect, was a dead loss."
"Then this time you shall have a real live wire,"
He smirked. They duly went back to their mire,
Where, as their new chief, they were appalled
To find a sharp-fanged water snake installed,
A tyrant who would pick on them at whim
And whom the fastest frog could not out-swim.
Helpless in the face of this oppression,
Nor daring to speak out, in secret session
They briefed a well-connected advocate
To urge the high-up honcho to abate
Their misery. But of this nothing came.
"They themselves," he thundered, "are to blame.
Why can't they just be happy as they are?
Learn this: what you wish for may be far
From what you want.  So think before you nurse
High hopes for change. Things might turn out much
    worse."

ATHENAE CUM FLORERENT AEQUIS LEGIBUS,
PROCAX LIBERTAS CIVITATEM MISCUIT,
FRENUMQUE SOLVIT PRISTINUM LICENTIA.
HIC CONSPIRATIS FACTIONUM PARTIBUS
ARCEM TYRANNUS OCCUPAT PISISTRATUS.
CUM TRISTEM SERVITUTEM FLERENT ATTICI,
(NON QUIA CRUDELIS ILLE, SED QUONIAM GRAVE
OMNE INSUËTIS ONUS) ET COEPISSENT QUERI,
AESOPUS TALEM TUM FABELLUM RETTULIT.

RANAE VAGANTES LIBERIS PALUDIBUS
CLAMORE MAGNO REGEM PETIERE A IOVE,
QUI DISSOLUTOS MORES VI CONPESCERET.
PATER DEORUM RISIT ATQUE ILLIS DEDIT
PARVUM TIGILLUM, MISSUM QUOD SUBITO VADI
MOTU SONOQUE TERRUIT PAVIDUM GENUS.
HOC MERSUM LIMO CUM IACERET DIUTIUS,
FORTE UNA TACITE PROFERT E STAGNO CAPUT
ET EXPLORATO REGE CUNCTAS EVOCAT.
ILLAE TIMORE POSITO CERTATIM ADNATANT
LIGNUMQUE SUPRA TURBA PETULANS INSILIT.
QUOD CUM INQUINASSENT OMNI CONTUMELIA,
ALIUM ROGANTES REGEM MISERE AD IOVEM,
INUTILIS QUONIAM ESSET QUI FUERAT DATUS.
TUM MISIT ILLIS HYDRUM, QUI DENTE ASPERO
CORRIPERE COEPIT SINGULAS. FRUSTRA NECEM
FUGITANT INERTES, VOCEM PRAECLUDIT METUS.
FURTIM IGITUR DANT MERCURIO MANDATA AD IOVEM,
ADFLICTIS UT SUCCURRAT. TUNC CONTRA DEUS:
≪QUIA NOLUISTIS VESTRUM FERRE,≫ INQUIT, ≪BONUM,
MALUM PERFERTE.≫ – ≪VOS QUOQUE, O CIVES,≫ AIT,
≪HOC SUSTINETE, MAIUS NE VENIAT MALUM.≫
    (1:II)

# Respect

Listen, Mister Nice Guy, please don't mess
With lowlife, even when it's in distress.
This geezer picks a snake up, stiff with cold,
And holds it gently near his heart of gold
To warm it up. Revived, it turns its head
And promptly bites its rescuer, who drops dead.
Another snake who sees this says: "Hey dude,
What you just done, to me seems a bit rude".
"Tough shit," the answer came, "he should have checked
Who he was dealing with, and shown RESPECT."

QUI FERT MALIS AUXILIUM, POST TEMPUS DOLET.
GELU RIGENTEM QUIDAM COLUBRAM SUSTULIT
SINUQUE FOVIT, CONTRA SE IPSE MISERICORS;
NAMQUE UT REFECTA EST, NECUIT HOMINEM PROTINUS.
HANC ALIA CUM ROGARET CAUSAM FACINORIS,
RESPONDIT: «NE QUIS DISCAT PRODESSE INPROBIS.»
(4:XIX)

# The lion's share deal

Don't think a business partner's like a mate
Or you may end up in a sorry state.

A case which illustrates this proposition
Concerns a certain hunting expedition,
In which a lion living in the wild
Was joined by three — by nature far more mild —
Farm animals: a cow, a goat and one
Poor sheep quite used to being put upon.
Working as a team they caught and slaughtered
One fine stag, which, as agreed, they quartered.
Then the lion said: "It's only fair
That as the lion I first take my share.
As jungle king I think I'm also due
A share as grateful tribute paid by you.
The third share I deserve because I'm worth it!
And the fourth? Well, who will dare to touch it?"
The moral of this tale you may rely on:
Never do a share deal with a lion.

NUMQUAM EST FIDELIS CUM POTENTE SOCIETAS :
TESTATUR HAEC FABELLA PROPOSITUM MEUM.

VACCA ET CAPELLA ET PATIENS OVIS INIURIAE
SOCII FUERE CUM LEONE IN SALTIBUS.
HI CUM CEPISSENT CERVUM VASTI CORPORIS,
SIC EST LOCUTUS PARTIBUS FACTIS LEO :
<<EGO PRIMAM TOLLO, NOMINOR QUIA LEO;
SECUNDAM, QUIA SUM FORTIS, TRIBUETIS MIHI;
TUM, QUIA PLUS VALEO, ME SEQUETUR TERTIA;
MALO ADFICIETUR, SI QUIS QUARTAM TETIGERIT.>>
SIC TOTAM PRAEDAM SOLA IMPROBITAS ABSTULIT.
   (1:V)

27

# The lion's ordeal

How are the mighty fallen, when they're jeered
By those by whom they formerly were feared!

Worn down by years, infirm and close to death
A lion lay. "He's drawing his last breath!"
The animals around thought gleefully.
A boar he'd once attacked then suddenly
Came rushing at the helpless beast to plunge
Sharp tusks into his body and expunge
That ancient grievance. Following close behind,
A bull with deadly horns charged the maligned
And hated creature. Finally an ass,
Seeing it was safe, as bold as brass
Turned round and gave him a contemptuous kick.
"Alas!" the dying lion whimpered, "Sic
Transit gloria. No beast in my day,
However proud, would such lèse-majesté
Commit. But now, when riff-raff dare defy
Me, well, I feel not once but twice I die."

QUICUMQUE AMISIT DIGNITATEM PRISTINAM,
IGNAVIS ETIAM IOCUS EST IN CASU GRAVI.

DEFECTUS ANNIS ET DESERTUS VIRIBUS
LEO CUM IACERET SPIRITUM EXTREMUM TRA-
HENS,
APER FULMINEIS AD EUM VENIT DENTIBUS
ET VINDICAVIT ICTU VETEREM INIURIAM.
INFESTIS TAURUS MOX CONFODIT CORNIBUS
HOSTILE CORPUS. ASINUS, UT VIDIT FERUM
IMPUNE LAEDI, CALCIBUS FRONTEM EXTUDIT.
AT ILLE EXPIRANS: «FORTES INDIGNE TULI
MIHI INSULTARE: TE, NATURAE DEDECUS,
QUOD FERRE COGOR, CERTE BIS VIDEOR MORI».
    (1:XXI)

## Sour grapery

A peckish fox looked up and saw a bunch
Of luscious grapes suspended from a branch.
"A juicy snack, just what I need!" he said
And jumped up at the fruit high overhead.
Alas, TOO high, for though he tried his hardest
Out of reach remained the tempting harvest.
Failure, though, the fox would not admit to.
"Huh!" he said. "Those grapes are quite unfit to
Eat, they're green." Take note those who get peeved
When their ambitions cannot be achieved.

FAME COACTA VULPES ALTA IN VINEA
UVAM ADPETEBAT SUMMIS SALIENS VIRIBUS:
QUAM TANGERE UT NON POTUIT, DISCEDENS AIT:
≪NONDUM MATURA EST; NOLO ACERBAM
SUMERE.≫
QUI, FACERE QUAE NON POSSUNT, VERBIS ELEVANT,
ADSCRIBERE HOC DEBEBUNT EXEMPLUM SIBI
   (4:III).

# Quid pro quo

Do as you would be done to, I'll buy that –
Till I get shafted, then it's tit for tat!

Here's a tale. A fox invites a stork
To come and share a meal and friendly talk.
The stork, who's worked up quite an appetite,
Arrives, but very quickly gets a fright.
For all there is on offer is a pottage
Served in a shallow bowl. How can he manage
To scoop this up with his long slender beak?
He goes home hungry, in a state of pique.
Later he returns the invitation,
But to his guest's considerable vexation
Brings out a spicy meal of chopped-up meat
Stuffed down a long-necked jar, a gourmet treat.
Though this is fine for him – he dines in style –
The fox can't reach the food, for all his guile.
Then when it seems he's at his wits' end
The stork laughs: "Chill out! Now we're quits, my friend!"

NULLI NOCENDUM : SI QUIS VERO LAESERIT,
MULTANDUM SIMILI IURE FABELLA ADMONET.

VULPES AD CENAM DICITUR CICONIAM
PRIOR INVITASSE ET ILLI IN PATINA LIQUIDAM
POSUISSE SORBITIONEM, QUAM NULLO MODO
GUSTARE ESURIENS POTUERIT CICONIA.
QUAE VULPEM CUM REVOCASSET, INTRITO CIBO
PLENAM LAGONAM POSUIT : HUIC ROSTRUM INSERENS
SATIATUR IPSA ET TORQUET CONVIVAM FAME.
QUAE CUM LAGONAE COLLUM FRUSTRA LAMBERET,
PEREGRINAM SIC LOCUTAM VOLUCREM ACCEPIMUS:
≪SUA QUISQUE EXEMPLA DEBET AEQUO ANIMO PATI≫
   (1:XXVI).

# Quid – no quo

People in high places should not turn
On those low down, who may be quick to learn
Clever tactics when they have a grievance,
And cause the mighty to get their comeuppance.
Once, to give her chicks a tasty snack,
An eagle seized some fox cubs and flew back
Straight to her eyrie, high up in a tree.
Distraught, the wretched vixen cried: "Please free
My babies, I implore you as a mother!"
"Go to hell," the eagle answered, rather
Rudely, feeling safe up in her nest.
And so the vixen set off on a quest
And came across a temple, where she found
Some flaming torches. Placing these around
The tree, she thought: "If those whom I so cherish
Have to die, then those will also perish
Holding them in thrall." And suddenly,
The eagle, with the tables turned, saw she,
Along with her own brood, was under threat
Of death. Now supplicant herself, "No! Wait!"
She pleaded. "Can't we make a deal? A quid
Pro quo? Please take your cubs. For what I did
I'm sorry." Thus the cubs were saved, although
The chicks went hungry. So: all quid – no quo!

QUAMVIS SUBLIMES DEBENT HUMILES METUERE,
VINDICTA DOCILE QUIA PATET SOLLERTIAE.
VULPINOS CATULOS AQUILA QUONDAM SUSTULIT
NIDOQUE POSUIT PULLIS, ESCAM UT CARPERENT.
HANC PERSECUTA MATER ORARE INCIPIT,
NE TANTUM MISERAE LUCTUM INPORTARET SIBI.
CONTEMPSIT ILLA, TUTA QUIPPE IPSO LOCO.
VULPES AB ARA RAPUIT ARDENTEM FACEM
TOTAMQUE FLAMMIS ARBOREM CIRCUMDEDIT,
HOSTIS DOLOREM DAMNO MISCENS SANGUINIS.
AQUILA UT PERICLO MORTIS ERIPERET SUOS
INCOLUMES NATOS SUPPLEX VULPI TRADIDIT.

    (1:XXVIII)

# Better dead than fed

How sweet is freedom! Hear this little tale.
A scrawny, famished wolf, far from hale
Or hearty, met one evening by the way
A plump and clearly well-fed dog. "I say",
He said, "You're looking in good nick. If I
May ask, how do you so well satisfy

Your body's needs? A wolf should be much stronger
Than a dog, but I'm now weak from hunger".
"Well, the answer's simple, mate – go find
A job," answered the dog. "A job? What kind?"

"Like mine. Security. You work at night
Guarding some geezer's house while he sleeps tight".
"Sounds just the thing for me! I've had enough,
My friend, of snow and rain and living rough.
I'd rather have a roof above my head and
Lots of food, glorious food, to hand."
"Then follow me", the dog said. But just then
The wolf observed some marks as of a chain
About the other's neck. "Hey, where did these
Come from?" he asked. A little ill at ease
The dog said: "Nah, they're nuffin'". "Even so,
Please tell me," said the wolf. "I'd like to know."
"Look, I'm a guard dog, innit? Which means I
Am fierce and scary, right? So they tie
Me up in daylight hours, then set me free
At dusk to roam about, just like you see.
But who's complaining? Look at the reward!
In return they give me bed and board,
The guv'nor chucks me bones from his own table,
Plus I get leftovers. So I'm able
To live okay and needn't shift my arse!
What's not to like, then, mate?" "Except, of course,
You can't just come and go at will. Correct?"
"Well, natch," the dog snapped. "What would you
    expect?"
"In that case I'll be off," the wolf replied.
"I may be starving but I have my pride.
No job, not even being king, for me
Would make up for the loss of liberty.
With due respect to guard dogs then, I'll say
Take care, my friend – and have a nice day!"

QUAM DULCIS SIT LIBERTAS, BREVITER PROLOQUAR.
CANI PERPASTO MACIE CONFECTUS LUPUS
FORTE OCCUCURRIT. DEIN SALUTATUM INVICEM
UT RESTIRERUNT: «UNDE SIC, QUAESO, NITES?
AUT QUO CIBO FECISTI TANTUM CORPORIS?
EGO, QUI SUM LONGE FORTIOR, PEREO FAME.»
CANIS SIMPLICITER: «EADEM EST CONDICIO TIBI,
PRAESTARE DOMINO SI PAR OFFICIUM POTES.»
«QUOD?» INQUIT ILLE. «CUSTOS UT SIS LIMINIS,
A FURIBUS TUEARIS ET NOCTU DOMUM.»
«EGO VERO SUM PARATUS: NUNC PATIOR NIVES
IMBRESQUE IN SILVIS ASPERAM VITAM TRAHENS:
QUANTO EST FACILIUS MIHI SUB TECTO VIVERE,
ET OTIOSUM LARGO SATIARI CIBO!»
«VENI ERGO MECUM.» DUM PROCEDUNT, ASPICIT
LUPUS A CATENA COLLUM DETRITUM CANI.
«UNDE HOC, AMICE?» «NIHIL EST.» «DIC, QUAESO,
    TAMEN.»
«QUIA VIDEOR ACER, ALLIGANT ME INTERDIU,
LUCE UT QUIESCAM, ET VIGILEM, NOX CUM VENERIT:
CREPUSCULO SOLUTUS, QUA VISUM EST, VAGOR.
ADFERTUR ULTRO PANIS; DE MENSA SUA
DAT OSSA DOMINUS; FRUSTA IACTANT FAMILIA
ET, QUOD FASTIDIT QUISQUE, PULMENTARIUM.
SIC SINE LABORE VENTER INPLETUR MEUS.»
«AGE, ABIRE SIQUO EST ANIMUS, EST LICENTIA?»
«NON PLANE EST,» INQUIT. «FRUERE, QUAE LAUDAS,
    CANIS:
REGNARE NOLO, LIBER UT NON SIM MIHI.»
    (3:VII)

# Oh deer!

Don't judge things only by the way they look;
You may think differently if you get stuck.

Drinking at a pool one day, a deer
Gazed at his mirrored image and thought: "Where
Would you find such splendid horns as mine –
So broad and strong, so elegant and fine?
My legs, though, let me down, being so thin
And spindly." Then with a start, he heard the din
Of hounds approaching – and he was the quarry!
Relying on those unloved legs to carry
Him away he swiftly reached the shelter
Of a wood. But there, amid the welter
Of twigs and branches, to his great dismay
His antlers got entangled, and no way
Could he break free. The hounds, soon finding him,
At once began to tear him limb from limb.
Dying, he moaned: "Oh, what a fool I am
To praise what's caused my downfall and then damn
What served me well. Now, too late, I see
How wrong I was. Oh dear! Woe is me!"

LAUDATIS UTILIORA, QUAE CONTEMPSERIS,
SAEPE INVENIRI HAEC ASSERIT NARRATIO.

AD FONTEM CERVUS, CUM BIBISSET, RESTITIT
ET IN LIQUORE VIDIT EFFIGIEM SUAM.
IBI DUM RAMOSA MIRANS LAUDAT CORNUA
CRURUMQUE NIMIAM TENUITATEM VITUPERAT,
VENANTUM SUBITO VOCIBUS CONTERRITUS

PER CAMPUM FUGERE COEPIT ET CURSU LEVI
CANES ELUSIT. SILVA TUM EXCEPIT FERUM,
IN QUA RETENTIS INPEDITUS CORNIBUS
LACERARI COEPIT MORSIBUS SAEVIS CANUM.
TUNC MORIENS VOCEM HANC EDIDISSE DICITUR:
«O ME INFELICEM! QUI NUNC DEMUM INTELLEGO,
UTILIA MIHI QUAM FUERINT, QUAE DESPEXERAM,
ET, QUAE LAUDARAM, QUANTUM LUCTUS HABUERINT».
  (1:XII)

41

# Dished

Don't treat a smart guy like a fool: you might
Turn out to be the one who's not so bright.

Dogs who live beside the river Nile
Won't stop to drink there lest a crocodile,
It's said, should grab them. So with canine cunning
They scoop up mouthfuls here and there while running.
Seeing a dog come near one day and take
A fleeting gulp, a croc said: "Hey, there! Make
Yourself at home and have a drink on me.
No need to be afraid. Relax! Feel free!"
"But after drinks comes dinner. I've no wish."
The dog replied, "to serve as the main dish."

CONSILIA QUI DANT PRAVA CAUTIS HOMINIBUS,
ET PERDUNT OPERAM ET DERIDENTUR TURPITER.

CANES CURRENTES BIBERE IN NILO FLUMINE,
A CORCODILIS NE RAPIUNTUR, TRADITUM EST.
IGITUR CUM CURRENS BIBERE COEPISSET CANIS,
SIC CORCODILUS: «QUAMLIBET LAMBE OTIO;
NOLI VERERI.» AT ILLE: «FACEREM MEHERCULES,
NISI ESSE SCIREM CARNIS TE CUPIDUM MEAE».
(1:XXV)

# A *fair cop, dove!*

Look out for schemers offering to defend
Your interests. You might come to a bad end.

A flock of doves! What hawk could ask for more!
Alas, not true for one such predator,
Who found his flying skills to be no match
For theirs, and so he never made a catch.
Convinced at last he wasn't quick enough
To beat them in fair flight, he turned to bluff.
"Listen, guys", he said, "I get upset
To think you all regard me as a threat,
And see how you are constantly on edge.
So how about we do a deal? I'll pledge
To give you my protection. What you do
Is make me king, with all the honours due
To royalty. Just put your trust in me,
And you can bill and coo contentedly
Henceforth". This to the peaceful doves appealed,
And soon the hawkish pact was signed and sealed.
But straightaway began a reign of terror.
Soon the doves discovered their great error,
For now their ruler used his power to ravage
One by one his subjects with his savage
Talons. "It's our own fault", moaned one dove,
So far surviving. "It's a fair cop, guv!"

QUI SE COMMITTIT HOMINI TUTANDUM INPROBO,
AUXILIA DUM REQUIRIT, EXITIUM INVENIT.

COLUMBAE SAEPE CUM FUGISSENT MILUUM
ET CELERITATE PENNAE VITASSENT NECEM,
CONSILIUM RAPTOR VERTIT AD FALLACIAM
ET GENUS INERME TALI DECEPIT DOLO:
≪QUARE SOLLICITUM POTIUS AEVUM DUCITIS,
QUAM REGEM ME CREATIS ICTO FOEDERE,
QUI VOS AB OMNI TUTAS PRAESTEM INIURIA?≫
ILLAE CREDENTES TRADUNT SESE MILUO;
QUI REGNUM ADEPTUS COEPIT VESCI SINGULAS
ET EXERCERE INPERIUM SAEVIS UNGUIBUS.
TUNC DE RELICUIS UNA: ≪MERITO PLECTIMUR≫.
   (1:XXXI)

# Might's right, OK?

A greedy wolf stood quaffing from a river.
Further down a lamb, all a-quiver
Being in such dangerous company,
Also slaked his thirst. And just then he
Got a real fright. The wolf for no good reason,
Other than a means to put the squeeze on
His poor neighbour, gave him a fierce glare
And growled: "Stop stirring up the water there,
You bleating idiot, while I'm trying to drink it!"
Trembling, said the lamb: "Oh, please don't think it
My fault, Mister Wolf, Sir. Honest. See,
The river flows past you first, and then me."
This hard fact being plainly evident
The wolf thought up a different argument.
"Six months ago," he snarled, "you bad-mouthed me;
I now demand a full apology."
"Six months ago," increasingly forlorn,
The hapless lamb replied, "I wasn't born."
"Then," roared the wolf, "perhaps it was instead
Your friggin' dad. Whatever, now you're dead!"
He then, with one determined brutal action,
Felled the lamb, and had his satisfaction.

You know how bullies are. They pick a fight
To get their way – and claim they're in the right.

AD RIVUM EUNDEM LUPUS ET AGNUS VENERANT
SITI CONPULSI; SUPERIOR STABAT LUPUS
LONGEQUE INFERIOR AGNUS. TUNC FAUCE INPROBA
LATRO INCITATUS IURGII CAUSAM INTULIT.
«CUR,» INQUIT, «TURBULENTAM FECISTI MIHI
AQUAM BIBENTI?» LANIGER CONTRA TIMENS:
«QUI POSSUM, QUAESO, FACERE, QUOD QUERERIS, LUPE?
A TE DECURRIT AD MEOS HAUSTUS LIQUOR».
REPULSUS ILLE VERITATIS VIRIBUS,
«ANTE HOS SEX MENSES MALE,» AIT, «DIXISTI MIHI.»
RESPONDIT AGNUS: «EQUIDEM NATUS NON ERAM».
«PATER HERCLE TUUS IBI», INQUIT, «MALE DIXIT
    MIHI.»
ATQUE ITA CORREPTUM LACERAT INIUSTA NECE.

HAEC PROPTER ILLOS SCRIPTA EST HOMINES FABULA,
QUI FICTIS CAUSIS INNOCENTES OPPRIMUNT.
    (1:I)

# Alas, last laugh

Hey, smartarse, with your fearless upfront wit,
Watch your back or you could look a twit.

A sparrow stood and chuckled while a hare
Fell victim to an eagle and the air
Resounded with his pitiable lament.
"Oops! I always thought you hares were meant
To be quick on your feet," the sparrow mocked.
"How come you're just about to be spatchcocked!"
His gloating, though, was suddenly cut short,
For he himself the eagle's eye had caught.
His desperate pleas for mercy were ignored,
And soon he too was summarily floored.
"I'm done for," said the hare, already half
Expired. "But – huh! — I'll have the last laugh."


SIBI NON CAVERE ET ALIIS CONSILIUM DARE
STULTUM ESSE PAUCIS OSTENDAMUS VERSIBUS.

OPPRESSUM AB AQUILA ET FLETUS EDENTEM GRAVES
LEPOREM OBIURGABAT PASSER: <<UBI PERNICITAS
NOTA,>> INQUIT, <<ILLA EST? QUID ITA CESSARUNT
    PEDES?>>
DUM LOQUITUR, IPSUM ACCIPITER NECOPINUM RAPIT
QUESTUQUE VANO CLAMITANTEM INTERFICIT.
LEPUS SEMANIMUS: <<MORTIS EN SOLACIUM!
QUI MODO SECURUS NOSTRA INRIDEBAS MALA,
SIMILI QUERELA FATA DEPLORAS TUA.>>
    (1:IX)

# Sorry, folks!

A mountain giving birth — what a palaver!
As the subterranean groans grew ever
More intense, this seismic parturition
Had the world agog with expectation.
But what popped out? A mouse! A sorry instance
Of promise somewhat let down by performance.

MONS PARTURIBAT, GEMITUS INMANES CIENS,
ERATQUE IN TERRIS MAXIMA EXSPECTATIO.
AT ILLE MUREM PEPERIT. HOC SCRIPTUM EST TIBI,
QUI, MAGNA CUM MINARIS, EXTRICAS NIHIL.
   (4:XXIII)

# Phaedrus & Co

**Gaius Julius Phaedrus** is notable for being the prime source in Antiquity of the fables attributed to Aesop. He wrote five books of them in verse, and similar poems thought to be by him have been identified, though some of the tales may be his own. As with Homer, scholars doubt if there was ever any one writer called Aesop, the name having become shorthand for a tradition of moral story-telling.

Phaedrus is believed to have been an educated slave from Thrace (an area covering parts of modern Bulgaria, Greece and Turkey) who was given his freedom by Rome's first emperor, Augustus. Born towards the end of the 1st century BC, he lived under four emperors and died around the middle of the 1st century AD.

In the prologue to his first book, Phaedrus says his aim is simply to amuse and offer good advice, though later on he acknowledges a fable can be an oblique way of saying something that you wouldn't dare say openly. Even so, on one occasion he managed to upset the emperor Tiberius's thuggish right-hand man, Sejanus, who had him punished; sadly, it's not known what he said.

Phaedrus chides literal-minded critics who jib at the idea of animals, and even trees, talking. "Relax," he says genially. "That's showbiz!" But of course the fables are really about human nature, which is why they are still entertaining and provocative after 2,000 years.

.......................................

Born and brought up in Pembrokeshire, **Towyn Mason** studied Latin up to School Certificate level and took a degree in Modern Languages (French and Italian) at Jesus College, Oxford. He lives in retirement in Highgate, after a career in journalism and broadcasting.

## Thanks ...

to **Isabel Raphael** and members of her *Latin for Pleasure* group for their encouragement, and to **Stephen Hodge**, president of the HLSI, and his committee for their support.

A huge debt of gratitude is owed to **Ken Brooks** for so generously making available his skill and his experience in book design to turn a crude assemblage of words and drawings into something fit for publication. No expression of thanks can come near to recognising the extent of his contribution, not to say his patience and good humour over many months and many changes of mind on the author's part.

Lightning Source UK Ltd.
Milton Keynes UK
UKOW05f0623070114

224084UK00002B/153/P